God's
Little book of

Comfort

Words to sooth and reassure
RICHARD DALY

WILLIAM
COLLINS

William Collins
An Imprint of HarperCollins*Publishers*
77–85 Fulham Palace Road
London W6 8JB

www.williamcollinsbooks.com

3 5 7 9 10 8 6 4 2

First published in Great Britain in
2008 by HarperCollins*Publishers*
This edition 2013

© 2008 Richard Daly

Richard Daly asserts the moral right to be
identified as the author of this work

A catalogue record for this book is
available from the British Library

ISBN 978-0-00-752834-9

Printed and bound in China by
South China Printing Co. Ltd.

Introduction

One of the basic needs for all humanity
is to be comforted in times of personal
sorrow or difficulty. Often that comfort
can come through words of support and
encouragement from special people in our
lives. However, there are times when we
are hungry for more, especially in times of
need. God is the one who is able to supply
all our needs; he promises us that if we
call on him, he will be there for us.

God offers comfort to all who are willing
to come to him. The invitation is extended
to everyone.

Jesus says in Matthew 11:28, 'Come unto me, all you who labour and are heavy laden, and I will give you rest.' This rest is not a temporary fix but a permanent solution; it is a complete rest for the soul.

This little book is designed to help you get in tune with this God of comfort and to lead you more fully to the one who is our 'very present help in time of trouble'.

Richard Daly

Replenish yourself

It's in the 'valleys' of your life that
you can drink from God's sweetest
streams. It's during this period when
he restores your soul.

For Further Reflection

Jeremiah 30:17
Psalm 51:12

Respect yourself

God tells us to 'love our neighbours as we love ourselves.' To love yourself simply means appreciating who you are in Christ.

For Further Reflection

Mark 12:33
Psalm 139:14

Overdo it

Find something to laugh about – a past memory or incident – and laugh so loud that your face hurts!

For Further Reflection

Genesis 21:6

Treasure pleasant moments

Isn't it comforting when you're lying in bed listening to the rain outside? Next time it happens, treasure the feeling!

For Further Reflection

Psalm 37:4

Let God lead

No matter what you're going through today,
you can count on God to be with you –
you can be sure he'll bring you through.

For Further Reflection
Isaiah 49:14–16

Live to your conscience

Comfort comes in knowing you've done the
right thing, no matter what people think.

For Further Reflection
2 Kings 22:2

Watch where you're heading

'Some people are so fond of ill-luck that
they run half-way to meet it.'

Douglas W. Jerrold

For Further Reflection
Psalm 18:10

Be assured

'Where there is sorrow there is holy ground.'

Oscar Wilde

_____

For Further Reflection
Isaiah 35:10

Find the lesson

Whatever despairing situation you may find
yourself in, the important question to ask is,
'Lord, what do you want me to learn
from this experience?'

For Further Reflection

Job 13:15

Discover God's plan

The reason God has brought you through so much is because he has a unique and specific purpose for your life. Get into his presence and discover what it is.

For Further Reflection

John 15:26
Jeremiah 29:11

Appreciate the struggle

Read Hebrews chapter 11. It contains many
of God's heroes; yet everyone of them had
their struggles. God can use your struggles
to make you strong.

For Further Reflection
Hebrews 11:34

Discover your weakness

Your limitations are God's opportunities
to get you to depend on him. In God's
eyes they serve a divine purpose.

For Further Reflection

1 Peter 1:7
Proverbs 17:3
Isaiah 48:10

What are you thinking?

'Nothing is miserable unless you think it so.'

De Consolatione Philosophaie

_____

For Further Reflection

Proverbs 23:7

Develop a positive outlook

Your attitude determines your behaviour. You choose whether to be happy or sad, thankful or grumpy. Choose a positive outlook today!

For Further Reflection
Ephesians 5:20
Amos 4:5

Soak it away

Next time you're feeling low, run a nice
hot bath, pour in your favourite bubble bath
and salts and soothe away your worries.

Let God in

God is personally interested in you. He wants
you to include him in all your areas of
your life. If you do, your plans will prosper.
What you plant will produce fruit.

For Further Reflection

Proverbs 3:6
Proverbs 16:3
Deuteronomy 8:18

Move forward

You are as close to God as you want to be.
The more you draw near to God the more
he will draw near to you.

For Further Reflection

James 4:8

Make the right choice

What you are today was determined by the decisions of yesterday. If you want to change your future, learn how to make better decisions today.

For Further Reflection

Joshua 24:15

Don't worry

Anxiety paralyses you and takes away
everything good in your life. Don't let it take
control, otherwise you'll end up immobilised.

For Further Reflection

Philippians 4:6–7
Psalm 56:3
Matthew 6:31–33

When God calls ... move

When God unexpectedly moves you to
speak words of comfort to somebody – do it.
It's about God's timing not yours.

For Further Reflection

Proverbs 11:30

Let go

When you can't understand – TRUST!

For Further Reflection

Deuteronomy 29:29

Stop and listen

In the business of your daily routine
remember God has a word for you. Be still,
and let God be God in your life.

For Further Reflection

Psalm 46:10

Appreciate your uniqueness

God's love for you is unlimited. If you were
the only person that needed forgiveness,
Jesus would have gone to the cross
just for you.

For Further Reflection
1 John 4:18

Come to daddy

'Abba Father' is an expression given to God. It means literally 'my daddy'. That's how intimate he wants us to be with him. How wonderful!

For Further Reflection

Romans 8:15

It's not by chance

You're not here today because you're lucky. You're here today because you're blessed! Take a moment to thank God.

For Further Reflection

1 Peter 5:7

Your chance shall come

'For the Lord himself shall descend from
Heaven ... and we shall be caught up to
meet the Lord in the air and so shall we
ever be with the Lord. Therefore comfort
one another with these words.'

For Further Reflection
1 Thessalonians 4:17–18

Accept Christ's invitation

In times of burnout, Christ offers us a permanent solution. He says, 'Come unto me, all you who labour and are heavy laden, and I will give you rest.'

For Further Reflection

Matthew 11:28–29

Hebrews 4:9

Consider yourself invaluable

In God's eyes your mistakes don't make you a failure, for in Christ you are always a success.

_____

For Further Reflection
Romans 8:38

Consider your troubles worthwhile

Whatever you may be going through,
remember what you suffer now will be
nothing compared to the glory
he will give you later.

For Further Reflection

Romans 8:18

Back to the future

Jesus is the same yesterday, today and
forever. You can't go back, but he can.
he can heal your wounded past and
break chains that had you bound.

For Further Reflection
Hebrews 13:8
Isaiah 65:17

Be transformed by the transformer

God is not content with your status quo. Every day in countless ways he seeks to mould and develop you into a greater likeness of his son.

For Further Reflection

Ephesians 4:1

Keep your eyes heavenward

Don't focus on the mountains that come up before you, rather focus on the mountain-mover. Nothing is too hard for him.

For Further Reflection

Mark 11:23–24

Be patient in trials

With God, waiting is not wasted time.
When you wait on the Lord,
he will renew your strength.

For Further Reflection
Psalm 37:34

Follow God's way

God can turn your rejection to redirection.
When one door is closed, he will always
open another. Watch out for it.

For Further Reflection
Revelation 3:8

Claim God's eternal love

God's compassion towards you never fails.
Each morning there is a renewed supply.
When you woke up you were surrounded
by a fresh outpouring of his love.

For Further Reflection
Lamentations 3:22–23

Consider yourself secure

When you seek God's protection, nothing can get to you without first coming through him.

For Further Reflection

Isaiah 54:57

Explore God's benefits

God has encouraging words you've
never heard, places you've never been
and joys you've never experienced.
Let him lead you today.

For Further Reflection
Proverbs 4:18

Don't give up

When it looks like there's no way forward
for you, don't stop short of the prize.
The greater the conflict, the greater the
conquest. The stronger the battle,
the sweeter the victory.

For Further Reflection
2 Chronicles 20:15
1 Samuel 17:47

Look for God's providence

No matter how bad things may look today,
his word to you is: 'The Lord himself goes
before you and will be with you. Do not be
afraid. Do not be discouraged.'

For Further Reflection
Deuteronomy 31:8

Carpe diem!

Seize the day! Appreciate the 'now'
moments of your life. Once passed,
they will never return.

For Further Reflection
Ephesians 5:16

Seek God first

Too often we talk to everybody
about our problems except the one
who can do something about it.
God says 'let your requests be
made known unto me.'

_____

For Further Reflection
Philippians 4:6

Involve God

When the picture looks bleak, don't ask God to take you out of it, but to join you in it. That way everything is transformed, including you.

For Further Reflection

Mark 4:39

Don't stay down

Proverbs talks about a righteous person
who may fall down seven times but always
gets back up again. You can be knocked
down but never knocked out!

For Further Reflection

Proverbs 24:16
Corinthians 4:8–9
Psalm 37:24

See weakness as strength

It's when you are at your weakest,
that God is able to make you a person
of power.

_____

For Further Reflection
2 Corinthians 12:9

Believe God

Don't fret about what other people think of you. What God thinks is what counts.

For Further Reflection
Zechariah 2:8

Take the first step

If you take a thousand steps away from
God, you only have to turn around towards
him. He's been following you all the way.

For Further Reflection

Luke 15:4
Luke 19:10

Live joyfully

Happy people rarely tend to think about happiness. They're too busy living it.

For Further Reflection
Proverbs 16:20

Seek power in prayer

'Seven days without prayer,
makes one weak.'

Anon

For Further Reflection
James 5:13–16

Let God fill you

God gives spiritual food to everyone –
except those who are full of themselves.

For Further Reflection
Proverbs 16:18

Accept God's view

You would worry less about what others
think of you if you realised how seldom
they do. Respect God's good opinion.

For Further Reflection
Psalm 139:17–18

Pass on the baton

To be appreciated is among the deepest
cravings of human nature. When you have
received it, dish it out to someone else.

For Further Reflection

Hebrews 13:1
John 15:12

God's plan can't fail

With God there's no such thing as a
'Mission Impossible'. When he sends you
on a mission, he makes sure you have
the means to succeed.

For Further Reflection
Luke 1:37

You're always on God's mind

God will never ever forget you. Your very name is engraved on the palm of his hand.

For Further Reflection
Isaiah 49:16

Keep going

It's when the burden seems heaviest, that
the breakthrough is near. Hold on for it.

_____

For Further Reflection
Galatians 6:9

Take time out

When you're under pressure – that's the
time to snatch a few moments to pause and
relax, reflecting on the goodness of life.

For Further Reflection

Psalm 46:10
Mark 1:35

Keep trusting

There is a rainbow in the soul for every
storm that comes your way. Faith is the
assurance that the sun will shine again.

For Further Reflection
2 Chronicles 20:20

Follow the light

God's word makes it clear that the way of
the cross will sometimes bring sacrifice,
suffering and loss. But he promises also
to walk by our side as our light for
the journey.

For Further Reflection
Matthew 10:39

Don't forget your blessings

Treasure the memories of all God has
done in the past – bring them to mind
as beacons of hope for the future.

For Further Reflection
Jeremiah 31:3–4

Be still

The Lord will not shout to get your attention. It's up to you to get away from the world's distractions to quiet your soul and listen closely to his still, small voice.

For Further Reflection
Isaiah 30:15

Bask in God's presence

In the shadow of doubt
in the depths of despair
in the struggle for hope
be assured God is there.

For Further Reflection
Genesis 28:15

Confess your sins

The crucified Christ who said
'Father forgive them for they know
not what they do' is the same Christ
who opens his arms wide with
forgiveness for you too.

For Further Reflection
Psalm 103:12

You're worth it!

The Lord doesn't see you as useless or
unworthy – to him you're not helpless.
You were worth Calvary's cross.

For Further Reflection
Psalm 13:5

Turn sorrow into joyfulness

Out of difficulties grow miracles.
Your disappointments are God's
appointments.

For Further Reflection
Psalm 30:11

Appreciate who you are

Don't compare yourself with others.
There are always greater and lesser people
than yourself. Value who you are in Christ.

For Further Reflection
Romans 8:17
1 Peter 2:9

You are who you are

You are unique. There is no one who is exactly the same as you. You are one of a kind, special, original and valued by God.

Don't throw in the towel

Being defeated is only a temporary condition. It's when you give up that it becomes permanent.

For Further Reflection

Matthew 24:13
James 1:12
2 Timothy 2:3

Keep pressing on

Striving towards your potential ought
to be your purpose in life.

For Further Reflection
Ecclesiastes 9:10

Look for the way out

Remember, you will never be faced
with a temptation that is too hard for
you to resist.

For Further Reflection

1 Corinthians 10:13
2 Peter 2:9

Wait on the Lord

A comforting thought is that no evil
will last forever or indeed for very long.
Whatever the trial ... 'it too shall pass.'

For Further Reflection

2 Corinthians 4:17
1 Corinthians 15:52

Keep your cool

Keeping your head when everyone around you is losing theirs is an example of peace.

For Further Reflection
Isaiah 26:3
Galatians 5:22

Face the fear

'Not everything that is faced can be
changed, but nothing can be changed
until it is faced.'

James Baldwin

For Further Reflection
Philippians 4:13

Build up your resistance

Tough times do not last.
Tough people do!

For Further Reflection
2 Timothy 2:3

Look at yourself

'The most difficult matter is not so much
to change the world as yourself.'

Nelson Mandela

For Further Reflection
Mark 8:36

Make the most of life

'Things work out best for people who
make the best of the way things work out.'

John Woode

For Further Reflection
Philippians 4:11
Hebrews 13:5

Remember the positives

Count your blessings – not your troubles.

For Further Reflection
Philippians 4:8

Value loved ones

The special people God has placed
in your life today are there for a reason.
Treasure them moment by moment.

For Further Reflection
Proverbs 17:17

You're a winner

To lose is not to fail. The only failure is
to lose and not try again. With Jesus
you can never fail.

Pray the serenity prayer

'God grant me the serenity to
accept the things I cannot change;
the courage to change the things I can,
and the wisdom to know the difference.'

Reinhold Niebuhr

For Further Reflection

James 1:5
Proverbs 4:5

Make the most of now

'To dream of the person you
would like to be is to waste
the person you are.'

Anonymous

For Further Reflection
Ephesians 5:20

Ask for power

Instead of asking for an easier life
ask God to make you a stronger person.

For Further Reflection

Isaiah 40:29

Psalm 29:11

Let go, let God

To cast your burdens on the Lord
means letting go and trusting God
for your next step forward.

For Further Reflection

Psalm 22:10
Proverbs 4:18

Let God lead

There are no hopeless situations.
In every misfortune God always has a
way out for you. Just hold his hand.

For Further Reflection

2 Samuel 22:31
Job 23:10

Get up!

It's OK to be down in the dumps.
Just don't stay there too long.

For Further Reflection

2 Samuel 12:22–23

Give it your all

When you know you've done your
best, God can't ask of you anything more.

For Further Reflection
Ecclesiastes 9:10

Believe God's truth

Sometimes we suffer more in imagination than reality. Bring your thoughts in line with the truth.

For Further Reflection

Proverbs 23:7
Psalm 117:2
James 3:14

Look for the silver lining

If there were no clouds we wouldn't appreciate when the sun comes out.

For Further Reflection

Matthew 5:45

Don't let fear stop you

Sometimes in order to overcome a weakness, even though you may feel the fear, persevere and do it anyhow.

For Further Reflection

Proverbs 3:25–26

Make the best of the situation

You can't control the cards life deals you, but you can control how you decide to play them.

For Further Reflection

Proverbs 3:5–6

Let God prune you

The pruning process can be a painful
one, but God knows what needs to be cut
back in your life. Trust him with the knife.

For Further Reflection

John 15:2

Turn failure into success

Some people grow through failure;
others never recover from it. See your
mistakes as stepping stones rather
than stumbling blocks.

For Further Reflection

Proverbs 24:16

Don't stay down

You must be like the lady who said, 'I'm never down, I'm either up or getting up!' Are you going to get up and try again?

For Further Reflection

Psalm 130:4

You're a new creation

The moment you accept God's forgiveness
you no longer 'have a dark past'. You have
a bright future.

For Further Reflection

Philippians 3:13
Psalm 51

Be anxious for nothing

Jesus said 'Can all your worries add a
single moment to your life?' Of course not!
Worry changes nothing.

For Further Reflection
Matthew 6:27

Reach the next level

God not only wants to forgive you of your sins – he also wants to cleanse you, heal you, restore you and give you complete victory.

For Further Reflection

1 John 1:7
Proverbs 28:13

Get your diploma of victory

As difficult as it may be, you are in
your present position for a reason. But you
are only there for a season. Take the tests,
graduate and move on to what God has next.

For Further Reflection

2 Corinthians 4:17

Let God work it out

For those who love the Lord, no
experience is ever wasted ... 'all things
work together for good to those who
love God, to those who are called
according to his promises.'

For Further Reflection

Romans 8:28

Get free in Christ

Unforgiveness creates a yoke that you
carry around wherever you go.
The power of forgiveness sets you free

For Further Reflection
Matthew 5:25

Tune into the master

God never changes. If he spoke to people
in the Bible, he will speak to you too.
Take time out to recognise his voice.

For Further Reflection

Revelation 3:20
John 10:4

Enjoy yourself

To be content is to announce 'I am what
I am. I cannot be anything other than what
God has called me. So I will be the best me
I can be. I will enjoy each day of me.'

―――――――

For Further Reflection
John 3:27

Patience is a virtue

Waiting is not easy, but it is necessary.
God is working on both ends of the line;
he's getting you ready for 'it' and he is
getting 'it' ready for you.

For Further Reflection

Habakkuk 2:3

Hang in there

When you finally decide to let something go you may feel empty for a time. This is normal. You are in between pain and the peace that will come.

For Further Reflection

Revelation 3:11
James 1:3

Replenish yourself

Stop regularly to recall God's goodness.
It restores your perspective and
strengthens you to face what's ahead.

For Further Reflection
Psalm 69:30

You're invincible with God

If God is with us who can be against us?
The presence of God tilts the scales forever
in your direction.

For Further Reflection
Romans 8:31

The four-letter word

Things getting you down? Too tired to pray?
Let me suggest one of a few four-letter
words God loves to hear us use ... HELP!

For Further Reflection

Jeremiah 33:3

Go back to basics

When was the last time you flew a kite, took a long walk in the woods, went on a bike ride, or just watched the sun set?

For Further Reflection
Ecclesiastes 12:1

Incline your ears to him

God is trying to tell you to be quiet,
be still and listen. Then, to move over
so he can take control.

For Further Reflection

Job 14:14
Psalm 40:1
Habakkuk 2:3

Rest in his arms

God says, 'I will hold you up', as long as you continue to lean on him.

For Further Reflection

Proverbs 3:4–5

Trust in God

Worry is incompatible with faith.
They just don't mix.

For Further Reflection
Hebrews 10:23
James 1:6

Stop the leak

Refuse to allow tomorrow's lagoon
of worries to drain into today's lake.
If you don't, you'll end up flooded.

For Further Reflection

Matthew 6:25–33

Live daily

Take one day at a time. That's the way
God dispenses life. He knows what will
work together for good.

For Further Reflection

Psalm 118:24
Proverbs 27:1

Down but not out

When you find yourself fallen down,
you're already in the best position to
reach out to God ... on your knees.

For Further Reflection

Psalm 145:14
Psalm 37:24

Cherish the unpredictable

'The only certainty is that nothing is certain.'

Pliny the Elder

For Further Reflection
Psalm 103:15–17

Trust and obey

Leaving the details of your future in God's
hands is one of the most honourable acts
of obedience you can do.

For Further Reflection

Psalm 37:5

It will work out

In the end, he will 'work everything together for good' and for his glory.

For Further Reflection

1 Corinthians 10:31

Relax

Soothing music has always had a
reputation for healing, tranquillising the
distressed and energising the weak. Listen
to something uplifting today and receive
a heart-warming experience.

For Further Reflection
1 Samuel 16:23

Look beyond the trial

We are never closer to the Lord,
never more a recipient of his strength
than when trials come upon us.

For Further Reflection

Psalm 34:18
Psalm 145:18

Open up to Jesus

When you are hurting, you need to
declare it to the Lord. Remember, he is
your 'wonderful counsellor'.

For Further Reflection
Isaiah 9:6

Something better will happen

Knowing that you have an eternal inheritance and a secure home in Heaven ought to help you rejoice through suffering.

For Further Reflection

James 2:5
John 14:1–3

Regress

Do something childish today, like going
to the local park and swinging on the
swings and sliding down the slide ...
it will soon get you giggling.

For Further Reflection
Mark 10:15

You're one of a kind

You are of infinite worth to God.
His love for you is as though you were
the only one living in this world.

For Further Reflection
Psalm 8

You're not an outcast

God draws near to the helpless, the undeserving, the destitute and all those who simply feel they don't measure up.

For Further Reflection

Luke 15:1–2

Psalm 85:6

Think highly of yourself in God's eyes

The next time you begin to think how unworthy and irrelevant and useless you are, remember that to God you are the object of his attention and his affection.

For Further Reflection

Zechariah 2:8
Psalm 105:15

Choose the best

There is no comfort like God's comfort.

For Further Reflection

2 Corinthians 1:3

Be dependent on him

Faith is counting on him when we
do not know what tomorrow holds.

For Further Reflection
Hebrews 11:1

You're surrounded

God promises ... 'I will go before you.
I will be on your right hand and on your
left, and my angels around about you,
to bear you up.

For Further Reflection

Numbers 11:23
Matthew 4:6

Surprise yourself

Watch out for those moments of surprised delight, like finding money in your coat from last winter. Those pleasant surprises serve a purpose!

For Further Reflection
Isaiah 58:14

Be more whole

Wounds cannot remain when the light of
God's love shines upon them. Absorb it
and feel its healing power.

For Further Reflection
Malachi 4:2

Endure

Expect troubles as an inevitable part of life and repeat to yourself the most comforting words of all: 'This too shall pass.'

For Further Reflection

2 Samuel 1:1

Take a deep breath

Fresh air gives you 66 per cent of
your energy. Love the open air ... it will
give you fresh life and zeal.

For Further Reflection

John 3:2

Reminisce

Treasure the moments where you received love. Those moments will survive long after your money and good health has vanished.

Listen to yourself

The doctor within is on duty night and day,
working to keep you fit. Give this doctor a
chance now and then ... listen to your body.

For Further Reflection
1 Corinthians 6:19

Gain strength in weakness

'The world breaks everyone, and afterwards
many are strong at the broken places.'

Ernest Hemingway

For Further Reflection
Psalm 34:18

Take a break

More people complain of insomnia,
panic attacks and tension headaches than
ever before. Accept Christ's invitation ...
'Come to me ... and I will give you rest.'

For Further Reflection
Matthew 11:28

Lose yourself

An hour's solitude enables you
to think more clearly and creatively.
It's a sure path to comfort.

For Further Reflection
Zechariah 2:13

Hope on

We all need hope. It teaches us that
adversity does not last forever.

For Further Reflection
Matthew 5:10–12

Bought with a price

No one is insignificant in the
eyes of the Creator. What he
creates he cherishes.

For Further Reflection

Genesis 1:31
Genesis 1:26–28

Keep moving

Don't give up when you are just moments away from victory. Your blessing may be just on the other side of your problem.

For Further Reflection

Lamentations 3:25–26

He's on your case

'Weeping may endure for the night
but joy comes in the morning.' Be
encouraged. God is working in the dark!

For Further Reflection
Psalm 30:5

Believe in yourself

When people reject you, it's usually
because they don't have the ability to see
the qualities inside you. They've bought into
a lie. Make sure you don't buy into it too!

For Further Reflection
Ezekiel 16:5–6

Freely receive, freely give

Until you care for yourself you won't really be able to care for anybody else. You can only give what you allow yourself to receive.

For Further Reflection
Matthew 10:8

God knows best

God knows you. He loves you and he has
a wonderful plan for your life. When you can
truly accept that, your healing will begin.

For Further Reflection
Jeremiah 29:11

Let your blessings overflow

Strive to leave a legacy that enhances
a positive memory and blesses those
you leave behind.

For Further Reflection
Psalm 112:6

Stick at it

Becoming a Christian is the work of
a moment. Learning to depend on God
is the work of a lifetime. You're still a
work in progress.

For Further Reflection

2 Corinthians 12:7–9

Grow from strength to strength

When you face tough times and come through them, you develop the faith needed to handle even tougher times.

For Further Reflection

Romans 12:3

Share your problems

Because you have a loving Heavenly
Father, whatever is important to you is
important to him too.

For Further Reflection

Psalm 27:10

Go to the top

If you want real help, go to the one who can give it. Jesus is the problem-solver, direction-giver, burden-bearer and the way-maker.

For Further Reflection

Genesis 18:14

Born for a purpose

Consider this:
You were born at just the right time
with just the right gifts to fulfil a plan
nobody else but you can fulfil!

For Further Reflection
Psalm 139:14

Protected 24/7

Not a single nagging, aching, worrisome,
gut-wrenching, blood pressure rising
thought escapes God's notice. You are
his personal concern.

For Further Reflection
1 Peter 5:7

Get out!

Walking is one of the best forms of
exercise. It puts a tingle in the blood,
promotes digestion, cleanses the mind
and elevates the spirit.

For Further Reflection
Jeremiah 6:16

Seek godly advice

The Scriptures declare: 'Don't let the sun
go down on your anger.' It's good advice.

For Further Reflection

Ephesians 4:26

Watch for the blessing

What you're struggling with right now is part of your preparation. Get ready – what the enemy meant for evil, God's about to turn it for good.

For Further Reflection
Genesis 50:50

The third person

Jesus promised before he returned to
Heaven that the Comforter would come –
the Holy Spirit. For this reason we are
never left comfortless.

For Further Reflection

John 14:6

Trust God's process

To experience true comfort is to sincerely believe that despite what you're going through, everything will eventually be OK.

For Further Reflection
2 Corinthians 13:11

Comfort someone

The mere act of comforting someone
has reciprocal effects. To comfort is
to be comforted.

For Further Reflection

Isaiah 40:1
1 Thessalonians 4:18

The wonderful counsellor

The only one person who can comfort
you the way you need to be comforted
is God. He is the God of comfort.

For Further Reflection

Psalm 34:18
2 Corinthians 1:3–5